WILLIAM & KATE
Royal Family

Marie Clayton

ATLANTIC WORLD

Introduction

The newest descendant of the royal House of Windsor, Prince George Alexander Louis of Cambridge, arrived in the world on Monday 22 July 2013. He joins a family that has seen many changes over recent years, both personally and in the way its members interact with the surrounding world. Although many long-standing traditions remain firmly in place, others have been abandoned or modified to create a modern royal family that is more in touch with contemporary life than ever before. The new baby may be a royal prince destined to spend his life in the relentless glare of the media spotlight, but he will also have far more of an opportunity to experience ordinary life than many royals before him.

The changes that are happening today began in a small way near the beginning of the last century. When Elizabeth Angela Marguerite Bowes-Lyon, youngest daughter of the Earl of Strathmore and Kinghorne, married Prince Albert, Duke of York, second son of King George V, she did not expect to become Queen. Even so, she had hesitated about joining the royal family because she felt the strict protocol of court life would prevent her from being able to speak her mind or do what she felt was right. Despite her misgivings Lady Elizabeth did accept Prince Albert and their wedding was held at Westminster Abbey on 26 April 1923; a first break from tradition, because previously royal weddings had been held privately in a royal chapel – and also, for the first time, the ceremony was recorded on film. The choice of bride also represented a change: although Elizabeth was a member of the British aristocracy she was not of royal blood and princes were still expected to marry a princess from one of the royal families of Europe. The Duke and Duchess of York began married life in their London home and a few years later started a family – Elizabeth Alexandra Mary was born on 21 April 1926 followed by Margaret Rose on 21 August 1930. Although there was interest in their birth there was no great media frenzy and the young princesses enjoyed a quiet family life – their uncle, Edward, Prince of Wales, was expected to become the next king and start his own family to continue the royal line.

In 1936 everything changed: after the death of King George V the Prince of Wales did briefly become King Edward VIII but within months had abdicated to marry American divorcée Wallis Simpson. As next in line the Duke of York reluctantly took the throne as King George VI and Princess Elizabeth suddenly became heir presumptive, instead of third in line of succession. However, if King George VI had later had a son, under the centuries-old law of primogeniture the boy would have taken precedence as a male heir even though he was much younger. Changes to the rules on the royal line of succession in 2013, just before the birth of their son, Prince George Alexander Louis, meant that William's and Kate's firstborn, whether a boy or a girl, would be third in line to the throne, behind Prince Charles and Prince William.

Right: *Looking radiant in a pale pink Alexander McQueen coat, Kate makes one of her last public appearances before the birth of the baby at Trooping the Colour on 15 June 2013.*

Opposite: *Kate was taken into St Mary's Hospital in West London early on Monday 22 July and Prince George Alexander Louis of Cambridge finally made his appearance at 16.24, weighing in at a healthy 8lb 6oz (3.8kg).*

Top left: *Lady Elizabeth Bowes-Lyon leaves her London home on the way to her wedding to Prince Albert, Duke of York, on 26 April 1923. In 1936 Prince Albert became King George VI after his older brother, Edward VIII, abdicated to marry Wallis Simpson, and Elizabeth became Queen.*

Top right: *Princess Elizabeth, aged two, with her nanny, Claire 'Allah' Knight. Eldest daughter of the Duke and Duchess of York, she was born on 21 April 1926 at the Mayfair house of her maternal grandfather, Claude Bowes-Lyon, 14th Earl of Strathmore.*

Above: *Princess Elizabeth and her younger sister, Princess Margaret, with the royal corgis Dookie and Janie playing at the Y Bwthyn Bach (The Little House) at Windsor in 1936.*

Above right: *The two young princesses were introduced to royal duties early – here they accompany their mother, Queen Elizabeth, to meet members of the Royal Company of Archers.*

Right: *King George VI inspects Princesses Elizabeth and Margaret in their uniforms in 1938. A Girl Guide company had been specially formed at Buckingham Palace so that Princess Elizabeth could socialize with girls her own age. A Brownie pack was formed for Princess Margaret since she was four years younger.*

The young Princess Elizabeth quickly adapted to her new life in the public eye, and photographs of her and Princess Margaret appeared at regular intervals. These were usually taken at official photo shoots or at public events attended by the royal family – there were very few candid shots or details of the royal private life of the type that are available of many members of today's royal family. The two young princesses did not attend a school with other children – they were both tutored privately at home and Princess Elizabeth later studied constitutional history and law with the Vice-Provost of Eton College and religion with the Archbishop of Canterbury as part of her role as heir presumptive. As a teenager she also began public duties and shortly after her eighteenth birthday was appointed a Counsellor of State during the King's absence, for the first time carrying out some of the duties of Head of State. In an effort to give her companions of her own age a special Girl Guide company was started at Buckingham Palace and the young princess later became a Sea Ranger. But it was the Second World War that really enabled Elizabeth to experience a similar lifestyle to other young women her age – in early 1945 she joined the Auxiliary Territorial Service (ATS) and by the end of the war had completed a course at No. 1 Mechanical Training Centre of the ATS and passed out as a fully qualified driver with the rank of Junior Commander.

Princess Elizabeth first met Prince Philip of Greece and Denmark in 1934 – they were distantly related through both Queen Victoria and King Christian IX of Denmark. In 1939, when the princess was still only a young teenager and the prince eighteen, they began exchanging letters regularly and the young princess soon declared that she had fallen in love. Despite the fact that Philip was a member of a European royal family the prospect of an engagement still caused much controversy; the Second World War made many Britons suspicious of foreigners, Philip was Greek Orthodox by religion, his

Above: *The crowned heads of Europe gather to celebrate the wedding of Princess Elizabeth and Lieutenant Philip Mountbatten on 20 November 1947. There had been some opposition to the wedding since Philip was a foreign-born prince of the royal houses of Greece and Denmark, but he had renounced his titles and became a British national before his engagement.*

family had strong links with Germany and he had very little in the way of financial standing. In the event Philip renounced his foreign titles, converted to Anglicanism and became a British citizen before an official announcement was made and he married Princess Elizabeth as Lieutenant Philip Mountbatten, becoming the Duke of Edinburgh on their wedding day.

The wedding itself, on 20 November 1947, was a low-key affair for such an important royal event – although it was still held in Westminster Abbey and attended by royalty and heads of state from around the world. Britain was in the process of recovering from the war, rationing was still in force and the bride had been obliged to save clothing coupons towards her dress – women around the country sent her their coupons to help. Crowds gathered to watch the bridal procession travel to the ceremony by horse-drawn carriage – and for the first time in history a royal wedding was broadcast live around the world, by BBC radio, with recorded highlights shown on television later in the day. In fact it was not until Princess Margaret married Antony Armstrong-Jones, on 6 May 1960, that a royal wedding was broadcast live on television – an estimated 300 million people worldwide watched the couple exchange their vows. By 1981, when Prince Charles married Lady Diana Spencer on 29 July, it would have been inconceivable that the event was not broadcast – and a record 750 million viewers worldwide tuned in to watch.

Princess Elizabeth gave birth to her first son, Charles Philip Arthur George at Buckingham Palace on 14 November 1948. But the Duke of Edinburgh – still a serving Royal Navy officer – was stationed in Malta for months at a time during the first years of his marriage and Princess Elizabeth lived with him when she could, so the young prince was left in England with his nanny, as was Princess Anne after she was born in 1950. In February 1952 King George VI died suddenly after a long illness; Elizabeth, staying in Kenya on her way to a tour of Australasia, was told the news by Prince Philip and the royal couple immediately flew home and moved into Buckingham Palace.

The new queen was welcomed as a breath of fresh air throughout Britain and across the Commonwealth. Just twenty-six when she was crowned, she was the youngest monarch on the British throne since Queen Victoria and she has introduced many changes to bring the royal family into the modern world. Her coronation, on 2 June 1953, was the first ever to be televised live from inside Westminster Abbey across the Commonwealth and afterwards she embarked on a series of foreign tours, visiting countries that had never before been able to welcome their reigning monarch in person. In 1958 she ended the custom of presenting eligible girls at court as debutantes and increased the number of garden parties held at Buckingham Palace so she had the opportunity to meet more ordinary people. Prince Andrew, born 19 February 1960, was the first child born to a reigning monarch for over 100 years, followed by Prince Edward, born 10 March 1964.

In line with royal tradition, as heir apparent Prince Charles was initially educated at home by a governess but at seven he was sent to Hill House School in Knightsbridge, becoming the first heir to the throne ever to attend a proper school. Later he went to the same preparatory school that his father had attended, Cheam, and then on to Gordonstoun – which he hated. Prince Charles was also the first heir to the throne to sit public examinations, taking GCE O and A levels. Now the precedent had been set, Princess Anne and the two younger princes also attended school.

Towards the end of the 1970s Prince Charles was approaching his thirtieth birthday and there was increasing pressure on him to marry. Several eligible ladies had come and gone and by now many of those who were around his age were already married. He finally choose the 19-year-old Lady Diana Spencer and their wedding, on 29 July 1981, attracted crowds to London to watch the procession to St Paul's Cathedral, while millions more watched the proceedings on television. Princess Diana had the gift of being able to connect with the people she met and she quickly won hearts around the world, soon becoming the most popular member of the royal family and subject to intense media scrutiny. Her youth and spontaneity often made other members of the royal family, who were much more constrained by protocol in public, appear rather cold and reserved – although this wasn't necessarily the case. But it was when she became a mother that Diana really brought change to the royal family, because she was determined that her boys would grow up experiencing the world that existed away from the palace.

Above left: *Prince Charles out for a stroll with his nanny in 1949. When he was born on 14 November 1948, Prince Philip was not in attendance – even royal fathers were not welcome in the delivery room, although it was only 13 years since a senior politician attended royal births by law to guard against substitutions.*

Opposite below: *Princess Margaret, left, and Princess Elizabeth, right, with baby Princess Anne at Balmoral in August 1951. Only six months later King George VI died and Elizabeth became queen.*

Above right: *The Queen and Princess Anne, with her pony Greensleeves, during the royal family's annual summer holiday at Balmoral in 1955. Apparently casual photographs like this were really the result of arranged photo calls.*

Below: *The royal family gathered at Frogmore House, Windsor, to celebrate the Queen's 39th birthday in April 1965. From left, Princess Anne, baby Prince Edward, the Queen, Prince Charles, young Prince Andrew and Prince Philip.*

Above left: *On 21 June 1982, just ten days before her twenty-first birthday, Princess Diana gave birth to her first child, Prince William Arthur Philip Louis, in the private wing of St Mary's Hospital, London, with Prince Charles present throughout the birth. The proud father tentatively holds his new son on the steps of the hospital.*

Above right: *The royal couple's second son, Prince Henry Charles Albert David – always to be known as Harry – was born on 15 September 1984.*

Right: *Princess Diana was determined that her sons would experience as much normal life as possible. A favourite day out was to Thorpe Park just outside London – here the princes are enjoying the rides with their mother in 1993.*

Below: *Prince William and Prince Harry at Polvier, the royal fishing lodge by the River Dee in Scotland, with their father in 1997. It was towards the end of this summer holiday that they heard the tragic news of their mother's death in Paris on 31 August 1997.*

The first child of Prince Charles and Princess Diana arrived on 21 June 1982: Prince William was the first royal ever to be born in a hospital and his father also broke with tradition by attending the birth. Diana was a devoted mother and when she and Prince Charles embarked on a major tour of Australia and New Zealand several months later baby William came too. It was in stark contrast to how things had been done previously – for generations royal children had been left behind with nannies for long periods while their parents travelled the world on tours of state. Although a few criticized Diana's decision, most ordinary people already understood that it was not acceptable to expect a mother to leave her child behind at such an early age.

Only a couple of years later, on 15 September 1984, Prince William acquired a brother: Prince Henry Charles Albert David, always to be known as Harry. Both parents wanted William and Harry to have as normal a childhood as possible; although Prince Charles had been to school his early education had been with a governess, but William's formal education began at the age of three at a nursery school in Notting Hill Gate, West London. Afterwards he attended a preparatory day school, and later Ludgrove Preparatory School in Berkshire, where he boarded part-time, coming home at weekends. At thirteen both William and later Harry went to Eton College, where many of the other boys came from a similar privileged lifestyle. To balance this Princess Diana privately took both boys with her on several of her unannounced visits to charities and institutions caring for the homeless and the dying, so they would be aware of others' suffering and that Britain was a multi-racial society in which not everyone was rich. And she taught both boys a valuable lesson about how to behave when meeting such ordinary people, stressing that each brief encounter might mean little to them but could represent a lasting memory for the other person – and that it was important to bend down if necessary to be on the same level as those they were talking to.

Awareness of everyday life was not limited to the downside – Princess Diana also took her sons on trips that other children of a similar age would enjoy: local amusement parks, Disneyland, cinema visits, queuing up at fast-food restaurants. For the first time candid photographs were available that showed a pair of royal princes looking relaxed and enjoying life, rather than standing formally and appearing rather ill-at-ease in front of the camera. After Princess Diana's untimely death, on 31 August 1997, her sons continued to value what she taught them – William still supports some of the charities he visited as a child and Harry has built a career for himself in the army, away from the spotlight as much as possible.

Below: *The princes share a joke at Highgrove in 1999 after Prince William, who had recently turned seventeen, had just taken his first driving lesson. Both young princes were currently studying at Eton College.*

Top left: *During his passing-out parade at Sandhurst in December 2006, Prince William struggles to hide his amusement as his grandmother inspects the troops. The Prince had completed a 44-week officer-training course.*

Top right: *The wedding of Prince William and Catherine Middleton on April 29, 2011 was cause for national celebration.*

Above: *The young couple arriving at Calgary Airport on 7 July during their 2011 tour across North America.*

Right: *The Duke and Duchess arrive for a dinner at Claridge's in May 2012. Kate wears a floor-length creamy white gown with a thigh-high slit by Roland Mouret and sparkling Jimmy Choo sandals.*

Opposite top left: *The Duke and Duchess of Cambridge during the Diamond Jubilee tour of South-east Asia in September 2012.*

Opposite top right: *On her second wedding anniversary, April 29, 2013, Kate visits Naomi House Children's Hospice. The Duchess's pregnancy had been announced unexpectedly early after she was taken to hospital with severe morning sickness in December 2012.*

Many people – not just in Britain but all around the world – watched William grow up into a charming and down-to-earth young man, and as he grew older there was increasing interest in whom he would choose as his bride. Many believed he would follow tradition and find a companion from a royal house of Europe or from an aristocratic family, but since Princess Diana had made sure that her sons were in touch with modern life perhaps it was not surprising that he chose a girl he met at university – just like many other young men. William and Catherine Elizabeth Middleton both started at the University of St Andrews in 2001 and it was not long before people began to take note that they seemed very close – although it was not until after Kate's attendance at William's passing-out parade at Sandhurst in December 2006 that she was established publicly as his girlfriend. When William and Kate married, on 29 April 2011, it was the first time a commoner had married a monarch-in-waiting for nearly 400 years – and the wedding was marked by all the finest pomp and ceremony for which Britain has always been so famous. More than 180 countries picked up the BBC live feed of the wedding in what was the biggest TV event in history to date – and the ceremony was also broadcast live on the Internet on both the BBC website and on YouTube, another royal precedent.

The first major event in the royal life of the new Duke and Duchess of Cambridge was an 11-day North American tour in July 2011. It was the first time that Kate had experienced the level of interest that a royal tour generates – heightened by the fact that everybody was keen to see the new young couple – but despite this she seemed happy and relaxed. The tour was almost as much of a new experience for Prince William – during the previous years a deal with the media had mostly kept him out of the spotlight and since leaving university he had sought to follow a more normal lifestyle by signing up for a three-year tour of duty and building a successful career in the army as a search and rescue helicopter pilot. In 2012 the young couple were in the spotlight again when, for only the second time in its history, the UK celebrated the Diamond Jubilee of a monarch when Her Majesty Queen Elizabeth II reached the 60th anniversary of her accession to the throne. Prince William, Kate and Prince Harry were in attendance throughout the whole Jubilee weekend, most memorably at the Buckingham Palace concert where they were pictured singing along with the crowd and waving Union Jack flags. The Duke and Duchess of Cambridge also embarked on a Diamond Jubilee tour of South-east Asia in September 2012 on behalf of Her Majesty the Queen.

This is the story of a new royal family, starting with William and Kate's spectacular wedding, following Kate as she takes up royal duties, and including the birth of the couple's first child. As expected, public and media attention through this period has been intense – but Kate has adapted perfectly to her role in the public eye and has support from her loving family – and Diana's legacy is also that William is more a man of the people than his father, with his more formal upbringing, could ever be. And William and Kate also have each other – this book not only reveals a little about a new royal family, but also shows a young couple who share many interests and a similar sense of humour, and are obviously deeply in love.

WILLIAM & KATE

Royal Family

A fairytale wedding

Above left: Kate Middleton waves to the crowds as she arrives at Westminster Abbey on Friday, 29 April 2011 to marry Prince William. She looked every inch a fairytale princess in her vintage-style ivory lace and satin dress by Sarah Burton at Alexander McQueen. The lace for the bodice and skirt was hand-made by the Royal School of Needlework at Hampton Court Palace. The bride's bouquet contained myrtle, lily-of-the-valley, sweet William, ivy and hyacinth. The myrtle came from a bush planted at Osborne House, Isle of Wight, by Queen Victoria in 1845 as well as from a plant grown from the myrtle used in the Queen's wedding bouquet in 1947.

Above right: Prince William chats to his Best Man – his younger brother, Prince Harry – as he waits for his bride to arrive.

Left: The Maid of Honour – the bride's sister, Pippa Middleton – takes charge of the bridesmaids and pageboys. Her figure-hugging dress quickly caught the eye of press photographers, and soon made Pippa almost as much a fashion icon as her sister.

Above left: Michael Middleton accompanies his daughter up the aisle. A former airline pilot, Michael and his wife Carole – a former airhostess – had left their jet-setting lifestyle after they began a family and set up their own very successful company selling goodies for children's parties. Kate had enjoyed an idyllic childhood, along with sister Pippa and brother James, growing up in a charming English village with devoted parents.

Above right: A beaming smile for her husband-to-be. William and Kate had largely ignored the list of dignitaries who courtiers suggested should be invited to the ceremony and had made their own guest list – which not only included foreign royalty, celebrities and sporting stars, but also friends from university, people from the bride's home village, and charity workers.

Left: William Arthur Philip Louis and Catherine Elizabeth make their marriage vows in front of the Archbishop of Canterbury.

Pomp and ceremony

Opposite above right and left: This was the first time a commoner had married a monarch-in-waiting for nearly 400 years – and the wedding was marked by all the finest pomp and ceremony for which Britain is so famous. It was Kate's idea that the aisle should be lined with an avenue of trees, to give a more informal countryside feel to Westminster Abbey's rather intimidating grey stone walls.

Opposite below left: The newly-weds emerge from the abbey.

Opposite below right: Carole Middleton and the Duchess of Cornwall.

Above: More than one million people packed London's streets to catch a glimpse of the happy couple, while the ceremony itself was watched on television by an estimated worldwide audience of two billion.

Left: Arriving at Buckingham Palace for the traditional appearance on the balcony overlooking The Mall.

Sealed with a kiss

Opposite above: Prince William and his newly titled bride the Duchess of Cambridge kiss on the balcony of Buckingham Palace.

Opposite below: The royal party appear on the balcony of the palace. From the left: Carole Middleton, Prince Charles, the Duchess of Cornwall with her grand-daughter Eliza Lopes, bridesmaids Lady Louise Windsor and Grace van Cutsem, Kate and Prince William, Lady Margarita Armstrong-Jones, page boys Tom Pettifer and Master William Lowther-Pinkerton, Queen Elizabeth and Prince Philip.

Above: After a buffet wedding reception for 650 people hosted by the Queen, Prince William drove his new wife from Buckingham Palace to Clarence House in a convertible Aston Martin belonging to Prince Charles. The car was decorated with red, white and blue ribbons and balloons, an L-plate and bore a number plate reading JU5T WED. The car was followed down The Mall by some of the prince's RAF colleagues in a Sea King search and rescue helicopter.

Left: For the evening celebrations at Buckingham Palace, Kate wore a second Sarah Burton creation, a stunning strapless dress with diamante beading at the waist, topped with a white fluffy shrug. She left Clarence House accompanied by the Duchess of Cornwall, in blue brocade, along with Prince William and Prince Charles.

Above: The day after the wedding the new Duke and Duchess of Cambridge left London by helicopter to spend the weekend in the UK, before the duke returned to work as an RAF search and rescue pilot the following week. The couple later went on a proper honeymoon to the Seychelles.

Opposite: Fresh back from their honeymoon, Kate chats to US First Lady Michelle Obama at Buckingham Palace on 24 May 2011, during the American president's state visit to Britain. Kate wears the Shola dress by high-street retailer Reiss – which promptly sold out after she was photographed in it.

Left: A first appearance together in the Royal Box at Wimbledon in June; the Duke and Duchess of Cambridge were on a private visit to cheer on Britain's great hope Andy Murray, who was battling Frenchman Richard Gasquet for a place in the quarter finals.

A day at the races

Left: Prince William and Kate chat to a friend at Epsom Racecourse in June. The Queen's colt, Carlton House, was running in the Derby – one of the classic races in the British equestrian calendar – and members of the royal family had turned out in force to cheer him on. Apart from the Duke and Duchess of Cambridge, the royal box included the Queen, Prince Philip, Prince Andrew and his daughters Princesses Beatrice and Eugenie, Prince Harry, the Earl and Countess of Wessex and Princess Alexandra.

Below right: Kate pictured while watching the race. Unfortunately the Queen's horse – which had been declared 5-2 favourite to win by the bookies – lost a shoe and came in a disappointing third.

Below left: Kate's smile to her husband says it has been a wonderful day out anyway.

Opposite: Kate attends the 10th Annual ARK (Absolute Return for Kids) Gala Dinner at Kensington Palace on 9 June 2011. She wears a stunning dusky pink cap-sleeve gown embroidered with Swarovski crystals, by British designer Jenny Packham.

On duty

Right: Camilla, Duchess of Cornwall, and Kate travel in an open carriage to watch Prince William make his debut on parade at Trooping the Colour. The ceremony of Trooping the Colour originates from traditional preparations for battle; colours, or flags, were carried, or 'trooped', down the ranks so that they could be seen and recognized by the soldiers as rallying points during the confusion of battle. In the 18th century, guards from the royal palaces assembled daily on Horse Guards to 'troop the colours', and in 1748 it was announced that the parade would also mark the Sovereign's official birthday.

Below: Sophie, Countess of Wessex, Princess Michael of Kent, Prince Harry, the Duchess of Cambridge, Lady Louise Windsor, Estella Taylor, Eloise Taylor and Margarita Armstrong-Jones stand on the balcony of Buckingham Palace after the Trooping the Colour Parade on 11 June 2011.

Opposite: Kate's long, glossy, chestnut hair is usually styled in a loose and natural way – a look that is now being copied by many other women.

Opposite: The Duchess pictured after a church service to mark Prince Philip's 90th birthday on 12 June 2011 in Windsor. With an admirable sense of thrift, Kate wears an azure blue jacquard coat-dress that she had previously worn to the wedding of her husband's friend, Nicholas van Cutsem.

Left: Kate enjoys a joke with the Duchess of Cornwall at the annual Order of the Garter service at St George's Chapel, Windsor Castle, on 13 June 2011. The Order of the Garter is the senior and oldest British Order of Chivalry, founded by Edward III in 1348. Membership in the order is limited to the sovereign, the Prince of Wales, and no more than 24 members.

Kate also has a good relationship with Prince Charles. At William and Kate's wedding reception, Prince Charles had been reported as telling another guest that he thought of Kate as the daughter he never had – a warm endorsement from her father-in-law.

Below: Prince William and Prince Harry play in the Sentebale Cup at Coworth Park on 12 June; William was playing for the Tusk Trust team while Harry played for the Sentebale side.

Visiting the Irish Guards

Above and left: On 25 June 2011, Prince William, who is Colonel of the Irish Guards, and the Duchess attend the Irish Guards Afghanistan Operational Medals Parade at Victoria Barracks in Windsor. Kate wore a smart double-breasted crepe navy officer's coat by Alexander McQueen as she and her husband presented medals to soldiers who had recently returned from serving in Afghanistan. William had only become Colonel of the Irish Guards in February 2011, and he wore the regiment's striking red dress uniform on his wedding day

A first royal tour

Right and below: Kate meets well-wishers during a walkabout following the wreath-laying ceremony at the National War Memorial on Day 1 of the royal couple's first North American Tour, which began on 30 June 2011 in Ottawa. She had diplomatically chosen a navy lace dress by Canadian-born designer Erdem for the occasion.

Kate and Prince William both seemed happy and at ease greeting the crowds who lined the route – even though this was Kate's first experience of the frenzied attention on a royal tour, and William had spent many years trying to retain his anonymity both at university and in the army. Prince Charles and Princess Diana's first tour together to Australia and New Zealand had been an exhausting baptism of fire for the new bride, but this time it seemed as if the newest member of the royal family was much more prepared.

Canada
Celebrates

This page: An estimated 300,000 people turned out to welcome the royal couple as they attended celebrations on Canada Day, which marks Canada's 144th birthday. Kate wore a stylish red hat with maple leaves – the emblem on the Canadian national flag – at the crown, designed by Sylvia Fletcher at Lock & Co.

Opposite above: Prince William has a private word with his wife during a visit to the Canadian Museum of Civilization in Gatineau, Quebec. They were attending a citizenship ceremony on 1 July – Canada Day – in which 25 men and women became full citizens of Canada and swore loyalty to Queen Elizabeth II.

Opposite below left: Meeting and greeting in Ottowa. It was obvious from the young couple's body language throughout the event that they were very much in love.

Opposite below right: Prince William is full of smiles as he prepares to make a speech – in both English and French. At one point he apologized for his French, saying 'It will get better as we go along'.

Learning new skills in Montreal

Below: In full cooks' whites – with Cambridge embroidered on the breast – William and Kate attend a cooking workshop and reception at the Institut de Tourisme et d'hôtellerie du Quebec. Prince William had insisted that some visits on the tour should be based around things that Kate would be interested in, and she clearly enjoyed making a soufflé with an Iles-de-la-Madeleine lobster.

Left: Kate was reported as having packed 40 different outfits for the tour – but she mixed designer outfits with those from her favourite high-street shops. Here she is eye-catching in a vivid purple Issa dress, while William sports a casual open-shirt look.

Opposite below left: The Duke and Duchess stand to attention in front of bearskin-wearing Canadian guardsmen during a parade for Canada Day. Kate's wrap-skirt cream Nanette dress is by Reiss; it features a cascading ruffle down the front, exposed zipper, overlapping petals on the skirt and three-quarter sleeves. She paired it with a stylish tasselled clutch bag by Anya Hindmarch.

Opposite above: Kate chats to some of the new Canadian citizens.

Opposite below right: William and Kate attend a youth reception at Rideau Hall in Ottawa. Their arrival brought the chattering among the 120 people present to an abrupt halt; the sudden quiet made William smile and he quickly joked, 'Talk among yourselves.' Kate's Issa bird print dress is a favourite – she also wore it the night before her wedding as she arrived at the Goring Hotel in London.

Above: The Duke and Duchess of Cambridge visit Rideau Hall, the Governor General's residence in Ottowa, to chat with veterans and their families. The young couple planted an eastern hemlock in the grounds, next to the pin oak that had been planted by Princess Diana and Prince Charles on 21 June, 1983 – which was William's first birthday. As an understated tribute to her husband's mother, Kate wore a grey dress from Diana's favourite designer, Catherine Walker.

Right: The royal couple visit a drop-in centre for homeless and young people in Quebec on Day 4 of their North American Tour, 3 July 2011. William had a game of table football, while Kate chatted to visitors and staff. They had spent the previous night on *HMCS* Montreal as it sailed along the St Lawrence River from Montreal to Quebec City.

Opposite: Kate looks professional in Montreal.

Above and opposite: Kate chose a jaunty knitted sailor dress by Sarah Burton at Alexander McQueen for a visit to Province House in Charlottetown, Prince Edward Island, on 4 July 2011, Day 5 of the tour. The cream cable-knit dress features a dropped waist and self-tying scarf, with navy bands accenting the hem, cuffs and collar. Province House was the location for the Charlottetown conference of 1864, where the idea of the nation of Canada was forged – but apparently the main reason Prince Edward Island was included on the tour is because it is also the setting for *Anne of Green Gables*, which is one of Kate's favourite books.

Left: At Dalvay-by-the-Sea on Prince Edward Island, the Duke and Duchess joined rival dragon boat teams that raced against one another. William's team won the dragon boat race – and Kate immediately threatened to push him in the water in revenge, which prompted a quick cuddle from her husband. The relaxed and intimate joking between the two delighted the watching crowds.

A nautical theme in Charlottetown

A moment together

Opposite: Kate and William look relaxed at Dalvay-by-the-Sea.

Right: During the day Prince William changed into his pilot's uniform to take part in a demonstration of a daring emergency landing procedure called waterbirding, in which a helicopter is brought down to land on water. Kate wrapped up warmly to cheer her husband on – and was even seen taking a few snaps of the event with her own camera.

Below: On July 4, the young couple took a brief private break from the tour and paddled a canoe across to tiny Eagle Island – known locally as Honeymoon Island – on Blatchford Lake, accompanied only by a local guide. That evening they enjoyed a 'trail supper' of caribou, berries and bannock bread as they watched a magical midnight tundra sunset. The following day it was back to work – with a visit to a Canadian Rangers Station on the lake, where they were pictured trying on matching red jackets.

A Western welcome

Opposite: The Duke and Duchess arrive at Calgary Airport on Day 8 of their tour of North America. Kate's lemon silk crepe dress by Jenny Packham had a very full, floaty skirt – which nearly caused an embarrassing 'Marilyn Monroe' moment on the very windy day. They were both presented with white Stetsons – the White Hat Ceremony is a traditional welcome to high-profile first-time visitors as a symbol of Western hospitality – but to the dismay of the waiting press neither Kate nor William put their hat on.

Right and below: Shouts of laughter and excitement from both William and Kate as they watch traditional Calgary Stampede activities at the BMO Centre on 8 July. They both look the part in their white cowboy hats teamed with jeans and casual shirts. Earlier William had thrown a stove into a 'chuck wagon', the traditional way to start one of the Stampede's races.

Lady in red

Opposite: A casual Prince William looks relaxed and happy. Although everyone was keen to see Kate during the trip he also had his admirers – and she had been careful neither to upstage her husband nor to hide in his shadow. It had soon become clear that theirs was a marriage of equal partners, who were truly in love.

Above and right: The Duke and Duchess sign the visitors' book at the ENMAX Conservatory at Calgary Zoo on July 8, where they had attended a presentation on science and technology. Kate later greeted children in the crowd waiting outside. Her red coat-dress is another outfit from designer Catherine Walker.

Welcome to the USA

Opposite: Kate and William chat together as they walk around Calgary Zoo. For many of her official engagements in Canada Kate wore a diamond maple leaf brooch, which had been lent to her by the Queen. The people of Canada had originally given the brooch to the Queen Mother in 1939 – the Queen had also worn it during her tour of Canada in 1951.

Right and below: After leaving Canada, the royal couple headed to California to be welcomed by California Governor Jerry Brown. At a summit to promote UK technological business interests in America they met delegates and then took part in a forum; there was laughter from the crowd when Kate tapped William – whose attention had obviously wandered – after the hosts asked for more opinions from the forum. The city's famous paparazzi photographers had been warned by LAPD Deputy Chief Michael Downing that their usual aggressive tactics would not be tolerated: 'It is really an honour to have the royal couple in Los Angeles, and we want to make sure they have a good impression.'

Duke and Duchess of Hollywood

Left: The Duke and Duchess of Cambridge stayed at the British Consul-General's residence in Hancock Park, Los Angeles, during their time in California. On 8 July the British Consul-General, Dame Barbara Hay, held a private reception in their honour – although one of the local TV networks had a helicopter overhead to transmit live shots of the event. The menu at the reception included such famous British delicacies as chipolata sausages and bacon-wrapped prunes – and to make the Brits feel really at home there were also Yorkshire puddings with roast beef and horseradish sauce.

Above: Prince William wore his favourite navy suit for the reception, but Kate chose the Maja green silk dress by American designer Diane von Furstenberg. Her bag is also by Diane von Furstenberg.

Opposite below: Prince William chats with David Beckham, who had been a guest at the royal wedding with his wife, Victoria. The guest list also included Stephen Fry, Lord Freddie Windsor – son of Prince Michael of Kent – film director Nigel Lythgoe and Bob Iger, chief executive of Disney.

The following day, 9 July, the royal couple visited the Santa Barbara Polo and Racquet Club for a polo match to benefit the American Friends of the Foundation of Prince William and Prince Harry. Prince William scored four goals in the game, cheered on by his proud wife, and his team won 5–3. At the end, Kate presented the winners with a cup – and received a kiss in return from her husband, to the delight of the crowd.

Glamour and Grace

Right: Hollywood may have its own version of royalty, but as the Duke and Duchess of Cambridge arrived at a BAFTA dinner in Los Angeles everyone wanted to speak to the real thing.

Opposite: Kate pulls off the Hollywood glamour look on the red carpet with a flowing, floor-length pleated lilac dress with a shimmering silver belt, designed by Sarah Burton for Alexander McQueen. Reporting on the event, *People* magazine said she brought 'glamour, grace and star power' to the event.

Left: Tom Hanks, Rita Wilson, the Duchess of Cambridge, Nicole Kidman and Prince William at the BAFTA 'Brits to Watch' event held at the Belasco Theater in Los Angeles on 9 July. The sense of excitement among some of the guests was such that Duncan Kenworthy of BAFTA felt compelled to urge them to 'be cool' and not all rush at once to meet William and Kate.

Right: Prince William stops to chat to the students as the royal party arrives in downtown Los Angeles's deprived Skid Row area to watch a dance performance at the Inner-City Arts academy. After the show William – who the previous April had spent a night sleeping rough in London for British homeless charity Centrepoint – and his wife left their handprints in clay as a memento. Kate's first effort barely left a mark prompting her husband to tease her: 'Come on, come on. Do it properly', showing her his own imprint and saying, 'Now, that's an imprint'. The couple then did a joint imprint, putting their hands over each other to push down – which prompted a bout of play fighting as they tried to push each other out of the way.

Below: William and student Jeysy Aguilar pictured during a ceramics class. The royal couple also tried their hand in a painting class – during which Kate gave her husband helpful painting instructions: 'William, do you know what you're doing? Start from the centre.'

Opposite: On the final day of the tour, Kate wore a navy and white crochet top from the high-street chain Whistles.

Help for heroes

Opposite above: As the final event of their North American Tour, William and Kate visited the Mission Serve: Hiring Our Heroes, an employment fair in the Culver City area of Los Angeles, aimed at finding jobs for military veterans. William and Kate helped to fill care packages for the children of deployed military personnel.

Opposite below: The veterans' employment fair was held in Studio 15 at the Sony Pictures Studio, and featured stands from major US employers. Prince William made a speech in front of a row of giant US and UK flags, in which he said that for him this was the most important part of the tour. He also made the audience laugh by referring to 'Harry, my low-flying, average, Apache-pilot brother'.

Above: As usual the Duke and Duchess are all smiles – although after 11 event-packed days she must have been ready to head for home. By that evening the couple were on a scheduled BA flight back to London, secure in the knowledge that their first overseas tour together had been a huge success.

A Family wedding

Left: Kate follows Sophie, Countess of Wessex, and Princesses Beatrice and Eugenie off the royal yacht *Britannia*, followed by Princes Harry and William. They had attended a private cocktail party the night before the wedding of Zara Phillips to rugby player Mike Tindall. Kate's outfit is the same Diane von Furstenberg Maja dress that she wore to the British Consul-General's reception in LA.

Below: Prince Charles and the Duchess of Cornwall, are followed out of the Canongate Kirk in Edinburgh by Prince Harry, while Prince William chats to Kate. Hundreds of well-wishers lined the streets for Scotland's first royal wedding in almost 20 years.

Opposite: Kate chats to her brother-in-law, Prince Harry. As the wife of the future King of England, Kate has already established herself as a fashion icon and designers would compete to provide her with outfits – but she has made it clear that she does not want to be just a 'royal clothes horse'. For Zara Phillips' wedding she chose an old favourite, an embroidered pale gold coat she wore in 2006 at the wedding of Laura Parker Bowles. It was simple but chic, perhaps chosen deliberately to avoid upstaging the bride, and set off with a tilted hat decorated with a rose and ribbons.

Left and opposite: The Duke and Duchess arrive to open the Oak Centre for Children and Young People at The Royal Marsden Hospital in London on 29 September. The centre specializes in treating children with cancer, and William is president of the Royal Marsden NHS Foundation Trust – the hospital is close to his heart, since it was here that his mother carried out her first solo royal engagement in 1982. The Prince made the visit even though he had been out all night on a search and rescue mission with his RAF helicopter unit.

Top: William and Kate make themselves comfortable on the bed of 14-year-old patient Digby Davidson.

Left: William chats to 7-year-old patient Ellis Andrews, in hospital waiting for a bone marrow transplant.

Supporting UNICEF

Right, below and bottom left: The Duke and Duchess at the UNICEF Global Supply Centre in Copenhagen, Denmark, on 2 November. The visit was to help maintain the spotlight on the ongoing humanitarian crisis in East Africa, which has left hundreds of thousands of children severely malnourished and at risk of starving to death unless they receive urgent help. The huge supply centre sources, supplies, packs and distributes the food, water, vaccines and emergency medical kits for children around the globe.

Back on duty

Opposite below right and below: Kate chats to locals as she and Prince William visit Summerfield Community Centre, in Birmingham, on 19 August 2011. The visit followed serious riots in the area the previous week in which three men were killed.

Left: Queen Elizabeth and her granddaughter-in-law attend a private viewing of Kate's wedding dress, which formed part of Buckingham Palace's 2011 summer exhibition. The dress was displayed on a headless mannequin – which prompted the Queen to remark that it looked 'creepy'.

Opposite and left: In October 2011 the Duke and Duchess were guests of honour at a fundraising Gala in aid of The Child Bereavement Charity at St James's Palace. William is a patron of both the fundraising organization and the charity itself. Kate's stunning red Sarai silk jersey dress is by Beulah, a company started by Lady Natasha Rufus Isaacs – daughter of the Marquess of Reading and a close friend of Prince William – to provide employment for human trafficking victims in India.

Below: Kate watches the Remembrance Day service from a balcony at the Foreign Office opposite the Cenotaph. The Queen laid the first wreath to commemorate members of the armed forces who have died fighting in all conflicts since the First World War, followed by Prince Philip, Prince Charles and Prince William (below). Prince Harry was in America on the final stage of his Apache helicopter training, so he attended his Army Air Corps squadron's remembrance service parade in Arizona.

And Harry came too

Left: Arriving at the National Memorial Arboretum Appeal at St James's Palace in London on 10 November 2011. The Appeal was launched in April 2009 by its Patron, Prince William, to develop the Arboretum into a world-renowned centre for remembrance and to ensure necessary facilities for the 300,000 visiting families, servicemen and women, veterans and members of the public each year. Kate wore a flowing pale silver chiffon Grecian-style one-shoulder dress by Jenny Packham; its relatively loose fit immediately led to speculation that she might be pregnant.

Below and opposite: The Duke and Duchess of Cambridge with Prince Harry attending the *Sun* Military Awards at the Imperial War Museum on 19 December, in London. It had recently been announced that Prince William was to serve in the Falklands and would be heading to the Search and Rescue Squadron at RAF Mount Pleasant shortly after spending Christmas with his wife. His six-week deployment was a solo one, so Kate had to stay at home – their first time apart since their engagement a year before.

Left and below: Prince Charles chats to his daughter-in-law and son as they arrive for the Gary Barlow concert in support of The Prince's Trust, at the Royal Albert Hall on 6 December. The Trust is raising money to help areas of London, Manchester and Birmingham hit by the summer riots. Kate had opted for a slightly more rock 'n' roll look for the event with a short Zara black and white printed dress – to show off those famous legs – teamed with a simple black Ralph Lauren jacket.

Opposite below left: Prince William looks happy with married life. In December it was confirmed that the Duke and Duchess of Cambridge would be undertaking their second royal tour, visiting Malaysia, Singapore, the Solomon Islands and Tuvalu. The tour was part of a wider programme that involved members of the royal family between them visiting every commonwealth country during the Queen's Diamond Jubilee year.

It was also announced that the couple would make Kensington Palace their family home. Princess Margaret's former apartment, the lavish four-storey, 20-room Apartment 1A – which comes complete with its own private walled garden – will need to be extensively renovated to make it fit for William and Kate, so they are not expected to move in until 2013.

Right: Kate and William dress casually for a visit to Centrepoint in London on 21 December 2011. Centrepoint is a national charity providing housing and support to improve the lives of homeless young people – at any one time, it works with over 500 young people providing a range of services to help them tackle the issues that can lead to homelessness. As a young boy the prince and his younger brother, Harry, were regularly taken by their late mother on private visits to Centrepoint hostels across the capital to better understand the lives of those less fortunate than themselves. The charity had become close to William's heart and he wanted Kate to see it in action.

Below right: William and Kate take part in a cookery class at Centrepoint, making low-fat festive mince pies and gingerbread. When Kate discovered that it was resident Tasha Barbi's 18th birthday she made a birthday cookie with an iced heart covered in hundreds and thousands.

A royal Christmas

Opposite above left: Prince Andrew and Prince Charles, followed by Prince William and Kate, head off to St Mary Magdalene church on the Sandringham estate on Christmas morning 2011.

Opposite above right: Kate looked very festive in deep red, teaming a simple knee-length frock coat with a hat by milliner Jane Corbett, who regularly creates pieces for the Middleton family. She also sported a pair of diamond drop earrings, which many believed were a Christmas present from Prince William.

Opposite below: A record 3,000 well-wishers waited outside the church to offer Christmas greetings to the royal family and police were on hand to manage crowds. Many were eager to hear news of Prince Philip's health – the 90-year-old duke had been admitted to Papworth Hospital in Cambridge after suffering chest pains and had been kept in over Christmas. He was finally released on Boxing Day after a minor operation.

This page: At Centrepoint in December 2011.

Opposite: Arriving at the UK premiere of Steven Spielberg's film *War Horse* at the Odeon Leicester Square on 8 January 2012 in London. Kate's figure-hugging lace Alice Temperley gown put paid to earlier rumours of a pregnancy – although they had not been officially denied, the word from royal experts was that the young couple were not yet ready to start a family. The premiere was held in aid of the Foundation of Prince William and Prince Harry.

Above: William meets some of the people involved in the making of the film. *War Horse* is an adaptation of Michael Morpurgo's classic 1982 novel of the same name, about a boy who tries to track down his horse after it is shipped away to serve in the First World War, and some scenes in the film apparently moved Kate to tears.

Right: The premiere was held on the evening before Kate's 30th birthday – William reached 30 on 21 June.

Flying solo

Opposite and below: Kate arrives at Alder Hey Children's Hospital to meet patients and staff in the hospital's burns and oncology units. She was dressed warmly in a belted chestnut-brown coat from Hobbs over a black high-neck jumper.

Left: Eight-year-old Jaqson Johnston-Lynch presents Kate with a posy of red roses and a Valentine's Day card during her visit to charity The Brink Bar on 14 February. The Brink, in Liverpool, is an alcohol-free bar run primarily to help people recovering from drink and drug addiction. Kate was in Liverpool visiting charities without husband Prince William, who was now on active duty in the Falklands.

Posted abroad

Above left and right: Prince William's posting to the Falkland Islands, as pilot on a four-man RAF search and rescue crew, came amid a diplomatic war of words between the British and Argentinian governments. The Argentinians claimed that the young royal had come in 'the uniform of a conqueror'. However, the Ministry of Defence said William's six-week posting to the remote outcrop, which Buenos Aires calls Las Malvinas, was part of a 'routine operational deployment'.

Left: Back home in the UK, Kate visited Rose Hill Primary School in Oxford, as well as Oxford Spires Academy, as patron of charity The Art Room. Kate's duck print coat dress, by Orla Kiely, was reportedly bought at half price in a sale.

Opposite above: The Queen, the Duchess of Cornwall and the Duchess of Cambridge are presented with hampers filled with gifts while visiting Fortnum & Mason in London on 1 March 2012. The Queen was very interested in a display of Diamond Jubilee United Services Tins filled with tea and clotted cream 'super digestives' (which don't disintegrate when dunked), which are being sent to 18,000 members of the armed forces to mark her 60 years on the throne. The store has been supporting the British military since the Napoleonic Wars, sending parcels filled with comforts from home to the troops.

Opposite below: The royal ladies all wore different shades of blue – Kate's coat is by Italian label M for Missoni.

Royal seal of approval

Left: Kate arrives at St Pancras station in London with the Queen and the Duke of Edinburgh to board a train to visit the city of Leicester. The royal visit to the city, on 8 March 2012, marked the first date of Queen Elizabeth's Diamond Jubilee tour of the UK, which covers every region of the country. The entourage took over an ordinary first-class carriage for the hour-long journey – which meant that Kate missed out on her first opportunity to travel in the royal train.

Below: The Queen and Kate watch a fashion show at De Montford University. The Duchess chose design student Becka Hunt from six finalists from the University to make her a pair of shoes to wear for the Jubilee celebrations. The winning shoes were in blue suede – inspired by Kate's engagement ring – with a delicate creamy white lace design.

Opposite: The Queen and the Duchess leaving Leicester Cathedral after attending a multi-faith service. Kate wore an elegant teal suit by L.K. Bennett and pillbox hat by James Lock, while the Queen was eye-catching in a cerise coat and matching hat by Angela Kelly.

Team work

Above and left: An estimated crowd of 5,000 waited to see the royal party in Leicester – and the Duchess of Cambridge took a back seat at most events since the focus of the visit was meant to be on the Queen. However, she still paused to chat to a group of guides and scouts and bent down to speak to a small child.

Olympic ambassador

Above: The Duchess and her father-in-law Prince Charles join in with children producing artwork during a visit to the Dulwich Picture Gallery on 15 March 2012. Kate, along with Prince Charles and the Duchess of Cornwall, visited the gallery to see work done by the Prince's Foundation for Children and the Arts.

Left: On the same day, in her role as Olympic Ambassador, Kate meets the GB Hockey Team at the Riverside Arena in the Olympic Park. The Duchess, who was hockey team captain at Marlborough College, was persuaded to try out the pitch for herself and promptly scored a goal. She was presented with a bespoke hockey shirt, as well as one for Prince William.

Jubilee celebrations

Above and opposite: Prince Harry, Kate and Prince William wave from the royal barge 'Spirit of Chartwell' during the Diamond Jubilee Thames River Pageant on 3 June 2012. A flotilla of one thousand boats accompanied the Royal family down the Thames, despite the appalling weather. Thousands of well-wishers from around the world flocked to London to witness the spectacular weekend celebrations, which included a star-studded free concert at Buckingham Palace, a carriage procession and a service of thanksgiving at St Paul's Cathedral. Kate was eyecatching in a bright red Alexander McQueen dress, topped off with a flamboyant red hat by Sylvia Fletcher from royal milliner James Lock & Co. She also wore a maritime-themed brooch with two silver dolphins that was a gift from the Royal Navy Submarine Service, of which William is Commodore in Chief, while the Strathearn tartan scarf honoured her Scottish title the Countess of Strathearn.

Left: Kate obviously has a fondness for vivid colours – for St Patrick's Day, when she visited the Mons Barracks in Aldershot to present members of the Irish Guards with traditional shamrocks, she wore an Emilia Wickstead coat in a deep blue-green.

Above: Queen Elizabeth II, Prince Harry, Prince Philip, Princess Beatrice, and Kate and William watch the traditional RAF flypast after the annual Trooping the Colour Ceremony from the balcony of Buckingham Palace on 16 June 2012. During the earlier carriage ride down The Mall Kate had nearly lost her stunning Jane Corbett hat – which matched the silver-grey dress by Canadian designer Erdem – due to strong winds.

Left: The Duchess wears an ultra-glamorous lavender dress by London Fashion Week designer Roksanda Ilincic to attend the UK's Creative Industries Reception, part of The British Government's GREAT campaign at the Royal Academy of Arts in London on 30 July 2012.

Opposite: William and Kate arrive for a British Olympic Team GB gala event at the Royal Albert Hall in London, on 11 May 2012. Despite the parade of celebrities at the event, Kate stole the show in the fashion stakes – her teal gown by Jenny Packham had intricate lace detailing, including a lace back panel studded with tiny gems. For once she dispensed with her standby LK Bennett pumps, opting instead for elegant diamanté Jimmy Choo sandals. She wore her hair up in a romantic plaited style, created by a team from the Richard Ward salon in Chelsea.

Right and opposite: The Duke and Duchess attend the service of thanksgiving for the Diamond Jubilee on 5 June 2012 at St Paul's Cathedral in London. Kate's dress, Alexander McQueen by Sarah Burton, featured dusty rose lace overlaid on white fabric – it was both elegant and fashionable.

Opposite below: The Queen, Prince William, the Duchess and Prince Harry stand on the balcony of Buckingham Palace following the Diamond Jubilee Procession in London on 5 June 2012. Prince Harry chatted to Kate during the event, several times making her smile – he has said he regards her as the sister he never had and that they get on very well.

Opposite above right: Kate and William leave the Signet Library in Edinburgh, after lunch on 5 July 2012. Later that day William was installed into the historic Order of the Thistle in a ceremony in Edinburgh attended by the Queen and the Duke of Edinburgh. This was Kate's first official appearance in Scotland since receiving the Scottish title Countess of Strathearn. She wore a primrose yellow Emilia Wickstead coat dress, accessorized with an Amanda Whiteley hat.

2012 Olympics

Above and left: William and Kate watch the cycling at the Velodrome on 2 August during the London 2012 Olympic Games. In the excitement of the moment they embraced after Philip Hindes, Jason Kenny and Sir Chris Hoy of Great Britain won the gold and set a new world record in the Men's Team Sprint Track Cycling final.

Opposite top: Kate and William, accompanied by Prince Harry, visit Bacon's College in Rotherhithe on 26 July 2012, to attend the launch of a new project to train sports coaches – an initiative to coincide with the London Olympics. For once William was dressed more casually on an official event, while Kate looked smart in a Hobbs belted dress and Pied a Terre wedges.

Opposite below: Kate sits alongside former hockey player Richard Leman (left), rower Katherine Grainger (right) and Dame Kelly Holmes during the Women's Hockey bronze medal match between New Zealand and Great Britain at Riverbank Arena Hockey Centre on 10 August.

Orchids in Singapore

Left: Kate pictured at The Istana, the official residence of the President of Singapore, on 11 September, the first day of the Diamond Jubilee tour of the Far East on which she and Prince William were representing the Queen. The tour covered Singapore, Malaysia, the Solomon Islands and the tiny Pacific islands of Tuvalu. In honour of the occasion Kate chose a silk dress from Singapore-born designer Prabal Garung.

Below and opposite: That afternoon William and Kate had visited Singapore Botanical Gardens to see the newly created orchid 'Vanda William Catherine' for the first time, as well as the white orchid that had been named after Princess Diana. The Princess had been due to visit Singapore to see her orchid, but had died before she had the chance. Kate's exquisite pastel-pink kimono-style dress, by British designer Jenny Packham, is covered with tiny hand-painted orchids that had taken a team of skilled artists at Chelsea firm De Gournay eight weeks to complete. William joked that the colours matched the orchids they had come to see.

Opposite: On a visit to the 'rain mountain' dome walk at Gardens by the Bay in Singapore on Day 2 of the tour. Thousands had arrived to greet the couple, who were there to plant a tree in the gardens before moving on to visit the Rolls-Royce campus. Kate had opted for a white broderie anglaise dress by Alexander McQueen, and looked cool and fresh despite the heat.

Above: On their last day in Singapore, 13 September, the couple visited Kranji Commonwealth War Cemetery and laid a wreath on behalf of the Queen and Prince Philip. Kate, dressed in a bespoke duck egg blue dress with a lace panel by Jenny Packham, carried a parasol against the sun as she and William walked through the rows of white graves, both solemn and deep in thought.

Right: The Duke and Duchess attending a cultural event and walkabout in Kuala Lumpur city park in Malaysia on 14 September 2012. A crowd of more than 10,000 had turned out to welcome them, which at some points caused Kate to look rather nervous although Prince William happily waved to onlookers.

Everything stops for tea

Opposite and left: Wearing an elegant ice-blue lace dress by Alice Temperley, with her hair pulled back in a bun and held in place with pearl-headed pins, the Duchess of Cambridge sips tea at a Diamond Jubilee party held at the British High Commission in Kuala Lumpur. She chatted to several guests, including shoe designer Jimmy Choo who later reported that they had discussed the importance of education for young people rather than shoes.

Below: The following day the royal couple arrived on the island of Borneo on the next stage of their Diamond Jubilee tour. Here they were able to enjoy a more relaxed time at the Borneo Rainforest Research Center in Danum Valley some 40 miles west of Lahad Datu.

Opposite: The Duke and Duchess on walkabout in Kuala Lumpur city park on 14 September 2012. Earlier that day Kate had worn the same dress – a pale grey chiffon design by Beulah London, which is run by the couple's close friend Lady Natasha Rufus Isaacs – for their first visit to a mosque. The royal couple look relaxed but that day a French magazine had published topless photographs of Kate snatched during a private holiday in the South of France and they were reported to be furious at the invasion of their privacy.

Above right: Kate arrives in the Solomon Islands wearing a bold print by Jonathan Saunders

Above left and right: The Duke and Duchess visit a cultural village in Honiara, Guadalcanal Island, on Day 7 of the Diamond Jubilee tour. Kate's bright yellow Jaeger dress, teamed with her signature LK Bennett pumps, looked cool and practical – and showed off toned arms and a developing tan.

Above: To reach the tiny Tuvanipupu Island, Kate and William travelled in a traditional canoe.

Opposite: On arrival they were greeted by village elders and a performance by traditional dancers. Kate wore a Mulberry navy collared fit and flare belted dress with Stuart Weitzman navy 'Corkswoon' wedges, but for once she was outshone by William who sported an eyecatching vivid pink shirt.

Left: On the last full day of the tour, William and Kate travelled to Tuvalu. In keeping with tradition, the couple were carried by the islanders from the airport to the welcoming ceremony in Funafuti, where William gave a speech on behalf of the Queen, who is still monarch of the islands.

A show of affection

Below: The Duke and Duchess chat with the England squad at the Football Association's new £100 million national training complex at St George's Park in Burton-upon-Trent on 9 October. After Prince William, who is President of the Football Association, had officially opened the new facility the young couple chatted and joked with the players, who were preparing for their 2014 World Cup qualifier against San Marino. Despite the chilly weather, Kate looked warm in a coat from high street retailer Reiss.

Left: William and Kate share a moment of affection.

Opposite: A bright smile from Kate as she and Prince William meet recipients of the Queen Mother Scholarship, the Diana, Princess of Wales Scholarship and the Duke and Duchess of Cambridge Scholarships at Middle Temple Inn in London on 8 October. The young couple have rapidly become the royal family's greatest ambassadors.

Opposite: : The news that the Duchess was expecting a baby broke suddenly in December 2012. She was less than eight weeks pregnant and the couple had not planned to make an official announcement for another month, but decided to end speculation after Kate was admitted to hospital with acute morning sickness. Three days later, on 6 December, Kate looked pale but happy as she left the hospital escorted by Prince William.

Below right: The Duchess of Cambridge arriving at Hope House, an all-female residential centre run by Action on Addiction for recovering addicts, on 19 February 2013. Chatting to one of the mothers at the centre, Kate admitted that she was nervous about giving birth.

Right: The royal couple enjoying the racing at The Cheltenham Festival on 15 March 2013. Kate looked cosy in a dusky-pink double-breasted Joseph coat, but retreated into the warmth of the private box after the second race. As they arrived several in the crowd had called out to ask if they should bet on a boy or a girl, but Prince William just smiled and told them to stick to horses.

Below: Braving the snow in March 2013, Kate spends the day outdoors as a Scout volunteer in the Lake District. She had been volunteering privately at her home near Anglesey since the previous January, but made a more public appearance to encourage other adults to volunteer.

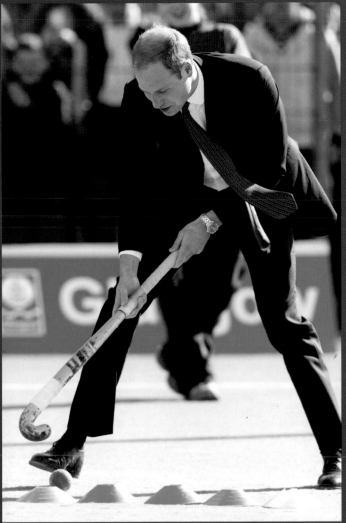

Baby on Board

Opposite and right: The Duchess of Cambridge joins Queen Elizabeth and Prince Philip, Duke of Edinburgh, on a visit to Baker Street Underground Station to mark the 150th anniversary of the London Underground on 20 March 2013. When presented with a 'Baby on Board' badge, Kate said she would be sure to wear it at home.

Above left and right: A keen hockey player herself, Kate laughs as Prince William – who also holds the Scottish title of Earl of Strathearn – participates in a hockey demonstration during a visit to the Donald Dewar Leisure Centre in Glasgow on 4 April 2013. The visit launched a new project for The Royal Foundation of The Duke and Duchess of Cambridge and Prince Harry, in partnership with Glasgow Sport and the Hunter Foundation, to encourage young people from the area to train as sports coaches.

Working their Magic

Above: Prince Harry, Kate and Prince William try out a little magic on the set used to depict Diagon Alley in the Harry Potter films. The three Royals, accompanied by children associated with the charities they support, were attending the inauguration of Warner Bros. Studios Leavesden on 26 April 2013. Kate displayed her thrifty sense of style by wearing a polka dot dress from high street store Topshop.

Left above: Prince Charles shares a joke with his daughter-in-law and eldest son during a visit to Scotland to open the new Tamar Manoukian Outdoor Centre. He had recently commented about becoming a grandfather for the first time, saying 'It's a lovely thought and I look forward enormously to that relationship.' – although he also said that the idea made him feel old. Kate, who was now around 6 months pregnant, wore a bright tartan scarf to keep out the bitter cold.

Left: Kate meets children during a visit to Naomi House hospice in Sutton Scotney, Winchester in April. Naomi House provides support to children with life-limiting conditions, and their families.

Family occasions

Right: On 22 May 2013, Kate made an unscheduled appearance at the first Royal Garden Party of the year, accompanying Prince Charles and the Duchess of Cornwall. The mother-to-be, who wore a pretty yellow and white check Emilia Wickstead coat-dress, chatted happily to guests and commented that the cooler weather had made her pregnancy more comfortable.

Below: Prince Harry and the Duke and Duchess of Cambridge on the balcony at Buckingham Palace during the annual Trooping of the Colour ceremony on 15 June 2013. The occasion marks Queen Elizabeth II's official birthday – this was also the last official engagement undertaken by the Duchess of Cambridge before the birth of her baby.

It's a Boy!

Opposite and above: Kate was taken into St Mary's Hospital in west London early on Monday 22 July and Prince George Alexander Louis of Cambridge finally made his appearance at 16.24, weighing in at a healthy 8lb 6oz (3.8kg). Prince William was present for the birth and like any proud father he immediately called the family to announce the news. When the new parents appeared on the steps of the hospital on Tuesday just after 19.00 to face the Press – many of whom had been camped outside for several weeks – William told reporters, 'I'll remind him of his tardiness when he's a bit older' and commented that perhaps they could all get back to normal now.

Left: Although news of the birth was first given in a press release, the traditional official announcement was also made by posting a proclamation on headed Buckingham Palace paper on an easel in the forecourt of Buckingham Palace. The easel was the same one used to post Prince William's birth 31 years earlier.

A hands-on father

Left: Prince William cradles his son. Catherine told reporters that he was a hands-on father and had already carried out his first nappy change.

Below: Before appearing in public the baby had already met many of his close family: Catherine's parents, Carole and Michael Middleton, had visited earlier on Tuesday afternoon, while William's father, Prince Charles, arrived with Camilla, Duchess of Cornwall later in the day. For her first appearance as a mother Catherine chose a crepe-de-chine blue and white polka dot dress by Jenny Packham and wore her sapphire engagement ring, which many took as a private reference to Princess Diana, who had worn a blue polka dot dress on the same steps to present baby Prince William for the first time and who had originally owned the ring.

Above: Catherine looked relaxed and happy as she smiled for the vast crowd of well-wishers who had gathered outside the hospital since the birth had been announced, although she commented that it was an emotional time, as any new parent would understand. At one point a tiny hand appeared from inside the blankets in what looked very like a wave, prompting a cheer from excited onlookers waiting for their first glimpse of the new prince.

Above: The baby's name was not officially announced until Wednesday 24 July – although this was faster than expected, since Prince William had not been named until 7 days after his birth, and Prince Charles nearly a month after his birth. When Prince George eventually comes to the throne he will be King George VII – or may choose to use one of his other names and be King Alexander I or King Louis I. The new baby is third in line to the throne, after his grandfather Prince Charles and his father Prince William, and will be known as His Royal Highness Prince George of Cambridge.

Opposite above left: Prince William joked that thankfully the baby had his wife's looks and 'way more hair than me'.

Opposite above right: Prince William leaves the hospital carrying his son in a car seat – and he passed one of the first rites of parenthood by fixing it into the car correctly first time. The couple spent their first night at home as a family at Kensington Palace, before leaving for the Middleton family home in Bucklebury, West Berkshire. Prince William had only two weeks' paternity leave from his job on Anglesey as an RAF search and rescue pilot.

Above: Crowds outside a floodlit Buckingham Palace. The Queen had earlier travelled to Kensington Palace to visit her third great-grandchild for the first time. It was also the first time in more than a 100 years that a reigning monarch was able to meet a great-grandchild in direct line of succession.

Over the last two years the partnership of William and Kate has charmed both the British public and many around the world. The birth of their son, Prince George, has made the couple into a genuine royal family, which it seems certain will take the House of Windsor securely forward into the future.

First published by Atlantic Publishing in 2012
This revised and updated edition published in 2013

Atlantic Publishing
38 Copthorne Road
Croxley Green
Hertfordshire
WD3 4AQ

ISBN 978-1-909242-16-6

Printed and bound in the UK